Arrest the

THE DOCTORS' OVER 60's
PROGRAMME

Arrest
the Ageing
Factor

•

JUDITH SWARTH, MS, RD
AND THE HEALTH MEDIA
EDITORIAL PANEL

foulsham
LONDON • NEW YORK • TORONTO • SYDNEY

foulsham
Yeovil Road, Slough, Berkshire SL1 4JH

ISBN 0–572–01827–4

Printed in Great Britain by
St Edmundsbury Press Ltd, Bury St Edmunds, Suffolk

Contents

Introduction

Older And Wiser: Nutrition Is Important

"Ageing begins with the moment of birth, and it ends only when life itself has ended. Old age is not a disease – it is strength and survivorship, triumph over all kinds of vicissitudes and disappointments, trials and illnesses."

It is not unusual to read about 60 year old marathon runners or 60 year old heart surgery patients. The number of older adults is increasing, with the number of adults 65 years old or older having doubled in the last 50 years. *(Graph 1, page 8)*

The older years can be active and rewarding. Illness and poor health are not an inevitable part of growing older. Many of the degenerative diseases that affect

Graph 1. Percentage Of The U.S. Population 65 Years And Older	
Year 1980 (1 in 25)	
1982 (1 in 9)	

One out of every nine citizens in the United States is above 65 years of age, and the percentage is increasing.

millions of older adults, such as cardio-vascular disease, cancer, stroke, osteoporosis, high blood pressure and diabetes, are related to lifestyle and diet.

Every part of the body undergoes natural changes with age, including the heart, lungs, brain, bones, muscles, skin, teeth, hair, eyes and ears. All cells in the body need a constant supply of vitamins, minerals, protein and other nutrients to function throughout life. Adequate nutrition is important to prevent and treat illness and harmful changes in our body tissues.

A person does not need to be a marathon runner to increase the chances for a long and healthy life. Simple changes in diet and exercise might prevent or treat several diseases and ensure the vitality and energy needed for an active body and alert mind. ARREST THE AGEING FACTOR will examine the many aspects of nutrition important to the health of body and mind of the older individual.

1

The Ageing Process

Some researchers believe ageing and death result from accumulated damage to cells over the years. This damage can be caused by toxic substances in the environment and in the diet, such as air pollution and some food preservatives. This damage can also be caused by toxins that result from normal body processes. According to this theory, the cells eventually stop functioning, organs become damaged and death occurs.

Other researchers believe that ageing is determined by genetics. The cells are programmed by the genetic code inside them to stop reproducing at a certain age and body systems slowly shut down until death occurs.

Stress accelerates the ageing process. Stresses include very hot or cold climates, nutritional deficiencies, disease, sedentary (physically inactive) lifestyle, smoking, and a life of hard physical labour.

Proper nutrition might be the best way to minimise the effects of ageing and the associated illnesses. Nutrition and other beneficial lifestyle habits reduce the effects of life's stresses and improve a person's chance for health and independence in later years.

The Changes Associated With Ageing

The years have a subtle affect on the shape and function of the body. Although these changes are inevitable they might be slowed, or in some cases avoided, by proper nutrition and health care.

At the microscopic level, changes occur inside cells. Cells are the basic building blocks of organs, bones, skin, and other body tissues. Waste products of cellular activity accumulate inside cells over the years and might interfere with normal cell function.

The genetic programming that regulates cell repair and regeneration becomes less efficient and cells misread their genetic material. As a result, cells produce the wrong molecules and body processes are impaired. Cells also stop reproducing themselves and some cells die. In addition, cell membranes become more fragile. When the protective barrier of a cell membrane is damaged, substances can enter the cell and cause further damage.

These changes in the health of individual cells affect organs and tissues. The body becomes less efficient in responding to hormones, the chemical messengers that regulate body processes. Muscles in the small and large intestines weaken, blood vessels become stiff, the heart pumps less blood, and less blood flows to organs. The kidneys filter fewer wastes and toxins from the blood and return fewer nutrients to it.

Fat is deposited in the liver, which hampers the liver's ability to work. Tissues draw fewer nutrients from the blood. The immune system weakens, which limits the body's defence against invading bacteria, viruses, and environmental toxins. The lungs hold less oxygen. Nerve signals relayed throughout the communication lines of the nervous system become more erratic.

In older adults who do not exercise,

muscle mass is gradually lost, more fat is stored, and bones weaken. Metabolism, which is all the physical and chemical changes that take place in the body, slows down by 12% to 20% in older adults. Decreased metabolism reduces calorie needs.

The changes in tissues and organs affect body processes. Digestion of food depends on intestinal fluids and digestive enzymes, which are molecules that break apart food substances in the stomach and intestines. As a person ages, the quantity of digestive fluids and enzymes decreases. This can cause digestive upsets and poor absorption of nutrients. In addition, the intestinal muscles are less efficient in later years and move food through the intestinal tract more slowly. Constipation can result.

Changes in the nervous system impair eyesight and hearing. Diminished senses of taste and smell make eating less pleasurable. Connective tissue is a substance that contributes to the tough, elastic quality of skin, tendons, blood vessels, and other tissues. As the body ages, connective tissues and skin become less elastic and gums are more susceptible to infection. The gradual loss of nerve and brain cells might decrease mental capacities and can cause memory loss and other behaviour changes.

Nutrition And The Ageing Process: Obtaining Nourishment In Later Years

The physical and mental changes of ageing are not inevitable. A nutritious diet is important during this time of life. Poor nutrition might accelerate the ageing process. One study of older adults showed that health was related to nutrient intake and that rates for illness and premature death were highest in people who consumed diets low in vitamins and minerals.

Studies show that older adults do not obtain the necessary vitamins and minerals for health. Obtaining adequate nourishment is difficult for older persons. The reduction in digestion, taste, and smell and problems with teeth and gums contribute to the difficulty.

Many older persons are socially isolated or live alone. Social companionship is as important to good eating habits as the diet itself. Shopping and preparing meals might be difficult for those with arthritis, physical weakness, or illness. Elderly people on fixed incomes might not buy nutritious food. Chronic illnesses, such as diabetes and kidney disease, require quite careful attention to diet that might be difficult for some people.

Elderly persons living in institutions might eat less if served foods they do not enjoy or if they are pressured to eat at designated times. Many commonly-used drugs interfere with nutrients in the body.

Malnutrition in older adults is a complex process that can include social, physical, emotional and economic factors. A nutritious diet during the later years can prevent or treat malnutrition and might improve some physical, emotional, and even social factors associated with aging. *(Table 1, Page 17)*

Table 1	Possible Signs Of Nutritional Deficiencies In Older Adults
Loss of appetite	Slow healing of wound, sore, or ulcer
Loss of taste or smell	Changes in skin colour (yellow, brown, grey)
Weight loss	Light sensitivity
Weight gain	Swelling of the legs
Pain or discomfort when eating or swallowing	Hair loss
Sore lips, tongue, or throat	Thin nails
Vomiting	Breathlessness on exertion and/or at rest
Regurgitation of food	Burning, pricking, pins and needles, or cramps in the legs
Change in bowel habits	Loss of balance
Diarrhoea	Confusion
Blood in the stools	Loss of memory
"Rash" (dermatitis) that does not respond to topical medication	Depression
Bleeding skin or easy bruising	

2
Nutritional Needs Of Older Adults

How Well Nourished Are Older Adults?

The physical, emotional and social demands of ageing affect the nutritional needs of the older adult.

The diets of older adults are often low in several nutrients, including protein, vitamin A, vitamin C, vitamin B_1, vitamin B_2, niacin, folic acid, vitamin B_6, iron, calcium and magnesium. Other nutrients likely to be low are the trace minerals chromium and zinc. Additionally, the adequacy of other minerals and trace elements has not been investigated. Also, older adults often do not consume adequate calories.

Women are more likely than men to be deficient in calcium and iron and men are more likely to be deficient in vitamin C, especially if they consume few fruits and vegetables. Those who do not eat several servings a day of fresh vegetables and fruit might be at risk for deficiencies of folic acid, vitamin A and potassium.

Older adults who limit their milk intake can lack adequate dietary calcium, vitamin B_2 and vitamin D. Older persons who are not exposed to sunshine might not produce enough vitamin D to meet their needs. Unless fortified milk is consumed, they might be deficient in this fat-soluble vitamin and at greater risk for developing osteoporosis and tooth disorders.

When consumption of whole grain breads and cereal is low, there might be chronic low intake of B vitamins and minerals. Processed foods and convenience foods used by the elderly are often low in vitamin E and high in fats, sugars and salt. Evidence shows that the higher the intake of fat, the shorter the lifespan.

One in four older women and one in five older men eat less than two-thirds of the calories they need for optimal health. In contrast, one-half of older women and one-fifth of older men are obese and weigh 20% more than they should. Undernutrition, too few calories and nutrients; and obesity, too many calories, and inadequate exercise are the two leading nutritional problems in older adults.

Nutritional Guidelines

Variety is the Spice of Life: Different foods are available throughout the year. These foods provide variety in colour, shape, texture, smell, and taste. They also provide variety in nutrition.

No one food or food group contains all the nutrients essential to health. Milk and milk products such as cheese, yogurt, and buttermilk provide vitamin B_2, calcium, protein, and vitamin A. But these products are low in other nutrients such as iron. Lean meats, chicken, fresh fish, and dried beans and peas provide iron and protein, but are low in calcium and vitamin D. Because of the unique nutrient spectrums, daily servings from each food group are recommended. These groups are whole grain breads and cereals, fresh fruits and vegetables, lean meats and dried beans and peas, and low-fat milk and low-fat dairy products. *(Figure 1, Page 21)*

Foods in the same group can contain different amounts of nutrients. Straw-

Figure 1. Recommended Daily Foods From The Four Food Groups

Group	Examples of Foods:	Servings	Household Measure
Dairy	Low-fat milk, low-fat cheese	2	16 fl.oz. 1 slice
Meat	Chicken +	1	3 oz./80g
	Peanut Butter	1	1 tbsp.
or	Lean beef, lamb, or veal +	1	3 oz./80g
	Dried beans and peas	1	3 oz./80g
Vegetables and Fruit	Broccoli +	1	3 oz./80g
	Tomatoes +	1	2 medium
	Orange juice	2	12 fl.oz.
or	Carrots +	1	4 oz./110g
	Spinach +	1	4 oz./110g
	Cantaloupe +	1	4 oz./110g
	Orange juice	1	6 fl.oz.
Breads and Cereals	Bread, enriched or whole grain	3	3 slices
	Cold cereal, fortified	1	1½ oz./40g
or	Whole grain roll +	2	2
	Rice, brown +	1	3 oz./80g
	Bread, whole wheat	1	1 slice

berries are a good source of iron but give little vitamin A; carrots are an excellent source of vitamin A but they contain little vitamin C; and potatoes are a good source of vitamin C but contain little folic acid. Variety in the diet guarantees that all the vitamins and minerals will be supplied.

Variety makes the diet enjoyable. Meals are more interesting with different tastes, aromas, and textures. Senses of taste and smell diminish with age and new flavours can stimulate taste buds and improve food consumption in under-eaters.

Whole and Unprocessed Foods: The closer foods are to their natural state, the more likely they are to contain more vitamins and minerals and less fat, salt and sugar than processed varieties. A processed food is any food that is tinned, frozen, dried or otherwise treated or "refined."

This does not mean processed foods should never be eaten. Many processed foods are nutritious, such as dried non-fat milk, frozen orange juice, and frozen peas. Some other processed foods, however, might have lost nutritional value during processing. For example, the high heat of canning destroys vitamin B_6, a nutrient low in many diets. White bread made with refined flour contains lower amounts of several vitamins and minerals as compared to whole wheat bread. White breads and white rice are also low in fibre, a dietary substance that prevents constipation and might reduce the risk of cancer, diabetes, and cardiovascular disease.

Many processed foods contain added fat, sugar, and salt. These nutrients are linked to an increased risk of developing cardiovascular disease, diabetes, hypertension, and obesity. The lower calorie needs of the older person leave less room for excess dietary fat and sugar.

A diet of whole and unprocessed foods contains several servings each day of fresh fruits and vegetables; dried beans and peas, lean meat, skinned chicken, or fish; whole grain breads and cereals; and low-fat milk and low-fat milk products.

Calories: Calories from food provide energy to the body. The body needs energy for processes such as heartbeat, breathing, maintaining the body temperature, and physical activity. Calorie needs decline between the ages of 46 years old and 75 years old. An individual needs 200 fewer calories in the daily diet to maintain ideal weight. Calorie needs decrease even more past the late 70s, when a person needs 400 to 500 fewer calories daily than were required in younger years. Calorie intake is balanced with energy needs if a person maintains a weight that approaches the ideal within five to ten pounds.

If a person consumes as much food as he or she did when younger, the result probably will be obesity. However, eating too little food can result in nutrient deficiencies. When calorie intake is less than 1,800 calories a day, the diet might be deficient in protein, calcium, iron, and vitamins.

Protein, carbohydrates such as starches and sugars, fat, and alcohol all provide calories. Older persons can meet nutritional needs by avoiding foods and beverages high in fat, sugar, or alcohol that provide few vitamins and minerals. Emphasis can be placed on lower calorie but nutrient-rich foods such as whole grain breads and cereals, lean meat, fish and poultry, dried beans and peas, fruits, vegetables, and either low-fat or non-fat milk products.

Protein: Protein is needed to maintain a strong immune system. Physical stress, such as illness or infection, increases the protein needs. If a person does not get enough calories, some protein is burned for energy, rather than used to build and repair tissues.

Adequate protein intake is important to maintain health, but excesses of protein increase losses of calcium and other minerals from bone and add to the risk of developing osteoporosis. If kidney function is poor, extra protein strains these organs.

Older people frequently consume inadequate amounts of protein-rich foods. In addition, protein needs might increase with age. Low protein intake can contribute to oedema, itching of the skin and related skin disorders, fatigue, muscle weakness, and loss of muscle. Low protein intake is often associated with vitamin and mineral deficiencies.

The diet should include four servings a day from the protein-rich food groups, such as lean meats, fish, poultry, dried beans and peas, tofu (soy bean curd), eggs, low-fat milk, yogurt, low-fat cheese, and buttermilk. Breads, cereals, and other whole grains also contribute protein to the diet, especially if combined with low-fat milk, dried beans and peas, or nuts.

Dietary Fat: Although small amounts of fat in the diet are necessary for the absorption of the fat-soluble vitamins and for healthy skin and hair, our diet is too high in fat. A high fat intake is associated with an increased risk of cardiovascular disease, cancer, and other degenerative disorders.

Fat comes in three main forms: saturated, unsaturated, and cholesterol.

Saturated fats are found in foods from animal sources such as meat, milk, cheese and eggs, and in vegetable fats such as palm and coconut oil. Saturated fats also are found in margarines and hydrogenated vegetable shortenings.

Unsaturated fats are found in peanut and olive oils, and in other vegetable oils, such as safflower, soy, and corn oil. Unsaturated fats also are found in chicken and fish.

Cholesterol does not supply calories or add body weight. However, cholesterol is associated with an increased risk of developing cardiovascular disease and is found only in foods from animal sources such as eggs, whole milk, beef, pork, luncheon meats, butter, and sour cream.

No more than 30% and no less than

Figure 2. Foods High In Fat

10% of calories should come from saturated or unsaturated fat to guarantee
adequate fat intake without increasing the
risk of disease. In addition to fatty meats,
dairy foods, and oils, many pre-prepared
convenience foods are high in fat, such
as frozen entrees and frozen vegetables in
sauce, luncheon meats, and bacon. Foods
lower in fat include dried beans and peas,
whole grain breads and cereals, fresh fruits
and vegetables, low-fat dairy foods, and
small amounts of lean meat, chicken, and
fish. (*Figure 2, above*)

How food is prepared can reduce or
increase fat and calorie intake. Foods that
are sautéed, fried, or served with sauces
and gravies can contain as much as twice
the calories from fat as those foods baked,
steamed, or grilled.

To further reduce the fat in the diet:

- Limit portions of lean meats, chicken, and fish to 3 to 4 ounces (100g), once or twice a day.
- Remove the skin before preparing chicken.
- Choose desserts that are low in fat, such as gelatin desserts, sorbet, meringue or yogurt and fresh fruit.
- Choose salad dressings made with low-fat yogurt, non-fat cottage cheese, vinegar, lemon juice, or other seasonings rather than oil.

Vitamins And Minerals

Increasing the vitamin content of the diet might improve health. Vitamins and minerals are important in all body processes. Several health concerns of older adults are related to poor vitamin and mineral intake. Poor intake is caused by a reduced capacity to digest and absorb vitamins and minerals; use of alcohol, or laxatives and other medications that reduce absorption or increase excretion of nutrients; and poor dietary habits. People with achlorhydria (low secretion of stomach acid) might not digest and absorb nutrients, such as iron. Some evidence suggests that changes occur with age that hinder the body's ability to use vitamins and minerals.

Older adults are at risk of deficiencies of vitamin A, vitamin B_1, niacin, and vitamin C. In one very large nutrition survey, one-half of the men and three-quarters of the women did not meet their daily vitamin A recommendation. Such deficiencies are associated with an increased risk of nervous, circulatory, and respiratory disorders. These disorders might subside when the lacking nutrient is supplied in the diet. Eye disorders in older adults, such as night blindness, are sometimes corrected by inclusion of vitamin A-rich foods in the diet.

Fatigue, confusion, disorientation, and depression are concerns of older adults. Poor absorption of vitamin B_{12} can result in marginal deficiencies of this nutrient and low blood levels of vitamin B_{12} are often found in the elderly population. When vitamin B_{12} is added to the diet, many of these symptoms disappear. Mental and behavioural disorders also respond to the inclusion of the other B vitamins in the diet.

A low intake of folic acid can cause

anaemia, bad concentration and weakness. The likelihood of developing anaemia increases with age. Folic acid deficiency is found in older adults, especially those who do not consume a daily source of fresh dark green leafy vegetables. Many medications commonly prescribed for older adults interfere with folic acid absorption and might encourage a deficiency.

One of the most common symptoms of a mineral deficiency is osteoporosis and its associated risk of increased bone fractures and jaw bone degeneration. Back bone degeneration caused by calcium loss from the bone is found in 80% of women over 65 years old. This bone loss begins in the 30s and progresses slowly throughout life. Poor dietary intake of calcium and limited exercise are linked to its progression.

The best way to avoid vitamin and mineral deficiencies is to consume a varied diet of fresh, nutritious, foods. *(Figure 3, Page 32)* In addition, a multiple vitamin and mineral preparation that contains the recommended dietary allowance (RDA) for all vitamins and minerals might improve nutritional status, especially for persons eating less than 1,800 calories.

Fibre: Fibre is the non-digestible part

of all fruits, vegetables, dried beans and peas, and whole grain breads and cereals. Fibre includes a variety of substances including bran in whole wheat bread, pectin in apples and fruits, lignin in grains and dried beans, and dietary gums such as guar gum, which is a thickening agent added to foods.

Different fibres can perform different functions in the body. A famous benefit of wheat bran and the fibre in dried beans is their ability to prevent constipation. These fibres bind to water in the intestine and improve elimination. Fibre in wheat and beans might prevent diverticular disease, a condition of painful, inflamed pockets in the walls of the colon. Fibres such as pectin, oat bran, and guar gum might reduce blood cholesterol levels.

Whole wheat bread, whole grains such as brown rice and oatmeal, bran flake cereals, dried beans and peas, and fresh fruits and vegetables are sources of fibre. Fibre is lost when grains are refined. Meats, fats, sugar, fruit juices, milk, eggs, and cheese are low in fibre.

Commercial bran products are high in fibre, but contain only one or two of the several types of fibre necessary for health.

Figure 3. Major Nutrients Supplied By Different Food Groups

Food Group   **Nutrients**

Fruits and vegetables

Vitamin A
Vitamin C
Folic Acid
Trace Minerals
Potassium
Fibre

Whole grain breads and cereals

Protein
B vitamins
Trace Minerals
Fibre

Low-fat dairy foods

Protein
Calcium
Vitamin D
(milk)
Vitamin B2
Magnesium

Lean meats, chicken, fish, dried beans and peas

Protein
B vitamins
Trace minerals

Too much fibre in the diet can interfere with the absorption of some minerals such as calcium, zinc, magnesium, and iron. This is not a problem unless large amounts of commercial bran are consumed.

Recommendations for fibre intake have not been established, but it is generally accepted that a diet that contains about 37 grams of fibre is beneficial to the health of all adults. This amount can be obtained from daily servings of the following.

- 6 servings of whole grain breads and cereals (1 serving = 1 slice of bread or 3 oz./80g cooked cereal or pasta) .... 13 grams
- 4 servings of fresh fruits and vegetables (1 serving = 1 piece of fruit or vege-table, 4 oz./110g) ....15–23 grams
- 1 serving of dried beans or peas (1 serv-ing = 5 oz./150g cooked) ......9 grams
Total .... 37–45 grams

Fluids: All body cells and organs need water to function. The blood needs water to maintain its volume. Water prevents overheating during exercise and the kidneys require water to flush wastes out in the urine. Adequate water helps prevent constipation and maintains moist skin and healthy hair.

The healthy adult needs about 6 to 8 glasses of water a day to maintain fluid balance. In addition, low-fat milk, soups, and fruit and vegetable juices are good sources of fluid. Some bottled mineral waters and club sodas are high in sodium and might need to be avoided on salt-restricted diets. Coffee, tea, and alcohol have a diuretic effect on the body and increase urinary excretion of fluids. They should not be considered part of the daily requirement for water.

Sugar: Sugar is a refined carbohydrate that provides calories, but does not provide vitamins or minerals. Because sugar requires several nutrients in order to be digested and used by the body, it uses more nutrients than it supplies.

Sugar is an easily recognised ingredient in desserts, but its presence in other foods, such as tinned and convenience foods and cereals, might go undetected. For example, ketchup is 30% sugar.

For the older person with low caloric needs, there is little room in the diet for sweets. No more than 10% of calories should come from sugar. In a diet of 2,000 calories, this allows one small dessert and a tablespoon of jam, honey, sugar, or other concentrated sweet. Jam, honey, and sugar should be used sparingly and sweet desserts should be consumed infrequently.

Caffeine: Caffeine both stimulates the

nervous system, aids concentration, and alters energy levels. Caffeine is found in coffee, black teas, cocoa and chocolate, soft drinks, and medications such as non-prescription pain relievers, appetite suppressants, and cold remedies. A person becomes more sensitive to caffeine with age and an excessive intake can cause jittery nerves, heart palpitations, or sleep problems. A sudden decrease in caffeine intake can cause headaches and fatigue. These symptoms can be avoided by a gradual reduction in caffeine intake. Instant cereal drinks, decaffeinated coffee and tea, low-fat milk, and fruit and vegetable juices are all good substitutes for the caffeine-containing beverages. (*Table 2, Page 36*)

Alcohol: For some people, a glass of wine might aid in relaxation and help digestion. Too much alcohol, however, affects overall health. Alcohol reduces the absorption of several nutrients, interferes with use of other nutrients, and increases nutrient losses. Nutrients that are likely to be depleted because of alcohol use include vitamin C, vitamin B_1, vitamin B_2, niacin, vitamin B_6, vitamin B_{12}, folic acid, zinc, magnesium, calcium, and potassium.

Alcohol provides calories, supplies no

Table 2	Caffeine Content Of Selected Beverages, Foods, And Medications
Item	**Milligrams Caffeine**
Coffee (5 fl.oz. cup), brewed, drip method	115
Tea (5 fl.oz. cup), brewed	40
Cocoa beverage (5 fl.oz. cup)	4
Milk chocolate (1 oz./25g)	6
Dark chocolate, semi-sweet (1 oz./25g)	20
Soft drinks (12 fl.oz. serving)	30.0–58.8
Nonprescription Drugs Alertness Tablets	100–200
Analgesic/Pain Relief	32–65
Diuretics	100–200
Cold/Allergy Remedies	16.2–30

vitamins or minerals, and depresses appetite. It irritates the digestive tract and increases levels of fats in the blood. If consumed in excess, alcohol can cause liver disease. *(Table 3, Page 38)*

Planning The Diet: A Summary

Guidelines for healthy eating must be individualised to meet the nutrient needs of each person.

A nutritious diet consists primarily of fresh fruits and vegetables, whole grain breads and cereals, and dried beans and peas, with at least two servings daily of lean meat, chicken, or fish and two servings of low-fat dairy foods. If fewer than 1,800 calories are consumed each day, a multiple vitamin and mineral supplement might be necessary to meet nutrient needs.

Dentures can limit the type and consistency of foods consumed. Foods such as fibrous vegetables can be mashed, chopped, strained, or puréed; sandwiches and lean meats can be cut into small pieces; and fruits can be sliced or lightly steamed for easy chewing.

If low-fat milk products are not well-tolerated another dietary or supplemental source of calcium and vitamin D must be found. Good sources of calcium include broccoli and dark green leafy vegetables; however, several helpings must be eaten to equal the amount of calcium in two servings of low-fat milk. A supplement that provides no more than 400IU of vitamin D might be necessary if milk is avoided.

If a person has digestive problems, food is less likely to irritate the system if several small meals are consumed rather than three large meals, warm to hot food is included at each meal, and the largest meal of the day is at lunch rather than dinner.

Table 3 Calories In Alcohol And Mixes		
Beverage	**Amount**	**Calories**
Beer	12 fl.oz.	140–150
Light Beer	12 fl.oz.	95
Dry Wine	3½ fl.oz.	87
Gin	1½ fl.oz.	97
Rum	1½ fl.oz.	97
Vodka	1½ fl.oz.	97
Whisky	1½ fl.oz.	97
Brandy	1½ fl.oz.	97
Mixes		
Club soda	8 fl.oz.	0
Ginger ale	8 fl.oz.	72
Cola	8 fl oz.	96

3

Nutrition And Special Concerns

Anaemia

The main function of the red blood cells
is to carry oxygen to the tissues. Within
each red blood cell is a protein called haemoglobin that contains iron. The iron in
red blood cells binds to oxygen in the lungs
and carries it to the brain, heart, muscles,
and other tissues. When a person is anae-
mic, the production of red blood cells is
reduced and the tissues do not receive an
adequate amount of oxygen. The result
is fatigue, poor concentration, anxiety, an
increased susceptibility to colds and other
infections, and reduced appetite.

Several dietary factors can contribute to
anaemia, including deficiencies of protein,
vitamin C, vitamin B_6, vitamin B_{12}, folic
acid, vitamin E, iron, and copper.

Iron deficiency anaemia commonly

results from lack of iron in the diet. Foods high in iron are lean meat, dark green leafy vegetables, dried beans and peas, dried fruit, potatoes, and whole grain breads and cereals. Diets low in calories are likely to be iron-deficient. Vitamin C-rich foods increase absorption of iron and should be consumed often with meals. Some substances in foods interfere with iron absorption, including the tannins in tea, oxalates in chard, and a compound in eggs. (*Figure 4, opposite*)

Folic acid deficiency is also common. Good sources of this B vitamin are dark green leafy vegetables (especially raw, since heat destroys folic acid), liver, asparagus, beets, legumes, citrus fruits, and whole grain breads and cereals.

Anaemia from vitamin B_{12} deficiency can occur in older adults because of a reduced ability to absorb the vitamin. A substance in stomach juices needed for B_{12} absorption is produced in lesser quantities as a person ages and less vitamin B_{12} can be absorbed from the diet. Ample intake of vitamin B_{12} is important to guarantee adequate absorption.

Figure 4. Foods High In Iron

Meats
Hamburger, cooked, lean
Lamb chop, grilled
Shrimp
Chicken breast, roasted

Non-Meat
Filberts (hazelnuts)
Pistachios
Cashews
Whole-wheat bread
Enriched white bread
Pinto beans, boiled
Spinach, raw
Raisins, seeded (Muscat)
Eggs
Bean sprouts
Broccoli
Romaine lettuce

Arthritis And Gout

Rheumatoid Arthritis: Rheumatoid arthritis is an autoimmune disease, meaning the body attacks its own tissues. This results in inflammation and swelling in the linings of joints, stiffness, and pain. Although any joint can be affected, those of the hands and feet are most often involved. With time, tissue surrounding bones and tendons is destroyed. This leads to crippling deformities and difficulty with movement.

A disturbed immune system, infection, and genetics might be involved in the development of the disease. Nutrition also might be involved. The pain and stiffness of arthritis increase when a person is badly nourished and improve when the person consumes a nutritious diet.

Malnutrition is common in people with rheumatoid arthritis. The inflammation of arthritis increases nutrient needs but lowers uptake of nutrients from the digestive tract. People with arthritis also have a difficult time preparing and shopping for food. In addition, steroid drugs used in treatment of arthritis cause calcium loss from the bones, which increases daily requirements for calcium and vitamin D to prevent osteoporosis. Regular use of aspirin to reduce inflammation interferes with vitamin C in the body and might cause gastric bleeding that can lead to iron deficiency and anaemia. Because of the interaction between aspirin and vitamin C, they should be taken at different times of the day.

Deficiencies of vitamin C, folic acid, iron, vitamin D, zinc, and vitamin B_6 occur in people with arthritis. Vitamin E and also selenium might be beneficial in treatment of this disorder.

Many of these vitamins and minerals are important to a healthy immune system. A well-functioning immune system might be important in the prevention or treatment of rheumatoid arthritis. Nutrients particularly important are calories and protein, zinc, iron, copper, selenium, vitamin A, vitamin E, vitamin B_6, and folic acid.

Dietary fat also might influence arthritis. Different types and amounts of fat in the diet affect levels of prostaglandins. Prostaglandins are hormone-like substances involved in the regulation of many body processes, including inflammation and immunity. The fat EPA (*See page 54*) might reduce levels of prostaglandins that cause inflammation.

A nutritious diet is important in the treatment of rheumatoid arthritis. Adequate intake of all vitamins and minerals improves a person's defence against disease and might also reduce pain and stiffness.

Gout: Gout is the accumulation of uric

acid crystals in and near joints. This accumulation causes swelling, inflammation, and pain. The likelihood of developing gout increases with age and is more common in men than women. Effective medications are available that flush uric acid from the body and help prevent attacks. A person with gout should consult a physician about proper therapy for this disorder.

For those with moderate to high levels of uric acid in the blood, dietary measures might help. Maintenance of proper weight can reduce a person's risk of developing gout. Alcohol raises uric acid levels, and gout sufferers should reduce or eliminate alcholic drinks. Uric acid is formed from compounds called purines found in some protein foods. Offal, sardines, mackerel, herring, and anchovies are especially high in purines.

Other meats, dried beans and peas, and fish contain lesser amounts. Low-fat dairy foods, fruits, and vegetables are low in purines. Nutritional or brewer's yeast, fat, and sugar also increase uric acid levels.

Behaviour And Nutrition: Nutrition plays a role in a healthy mind as well as a healthy body. It has been known for many years that an extreme deficiency of certain nutrients, such as vitamin B_1 and niacin, results in severe mental problems. New research indicates marginal deficiencies also affect a person's mental state.

Depression is not always related to nutritional habits; however, some nutritional causes of depression might include deficiencies of niacin, thiamin, or folic acid.

In recent years identification of a substance in the brain called serotonin has linked nutrition to sleep, appetite, and mood. Both high protein meals and low vitamin B_6 in the diet might reduce serotonin formation and cause sleep difficulties and depression. Serotonin levels increase and depression might disappear in some cases following supplementation with vitamin B_6. Low levels of serotonin are found in some suicidal patients. (*Figure 5, Page 46*)

Vitamin B_6 is found in protein-rich foods such as lean meats, fish, poultry, legumes, whole grain breads and cereals. Refined white bread and tinned foods contain little of the vitamin. Vitamin B_6 might cause nerve damage when taken at doses greater than 500 mg.

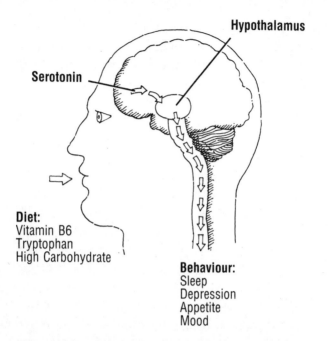

Hypothalamus

Serotonin

Diet:
Vitamin B6
Tryptophan
High Carbohydrate

Behaviour:
Sleep
Depression
Appetite
Mood

Figure 5.   Diet Might Affect Behaviour

In recent years identification of a substance in the brain called serotonin has linked nutrition to sleep, appetite, and mood.

The calming action of serotonin affects sleep patterns as well. In addition to the vitamin B_6, serotonin formation requires tryptophan. Tryptophan is an amino acid, one of the building blocks of protein. Using supplements of tryptophan with a high-carbohydrate, low-protein meal might produce a calming effect that helps people to fall asleep easily.

Memory also is affected by nutrition. Lack of vitamin B_{12} is associated with poor memory in the elderly. Impaired memory can be an early sign of the severe, progressive senility of Alzheimer's disease. Choline is a vitamin-like substance found in dried beans and peas, wheat germ, and offal that might be important in the health of the nerves involved in memory. The metal aluminium might interfere with reactions in nerve cells involving choline and be involved in development of Alzheimer's disease. Adequate dietary calcium might prevent the accumulation of aluminium.

Bones

Bones deteriorate when the diet is low in calcium and a person is sedentary. Over the years, the daily loss of calcium from the bones can result in osteoporosis. By the age of 70 many women have lost half of their bone mass and 40% of women have experienced spontaneous fractures. Fractures heal poorly in the elderly, especially when they are malnourished.

Fractures can lead to infections and even disability.

Factors that contribute to bone loss include lack of exercise, hormonal changes after menopause (decreased oestrogen), and dietary deficiencies. Nutrients needed to maintain healthy bones include calcium, vitamin D, phosphorus, magnesium, and flouride. Cigarette smoking, alcohol, caffeine, and excess protein and phosphorus are associated with thinning bones.

The recommendation for calcium is 1,000 to 1,500 mg a day to prevent bone loss. This is above the 500 mg most women consume or is suggested by the RDA. As a person ages, calcium is absorbed less efficiently from the digestive tract, which increases the importance of an ample intake of the mineral daily. An increased intake of calcium might not only prevent osteoporosis, but also might help regenerate some lost bone tissue. *(Table 4, Page 49)*

Vitamin D also protects against bone losses. Vitamin D deficiency is associated with soft bones, a condition called osteomalacia. Inadequate exposure to sunlight combined with aging kidneys that are less capable of manufacturing vitamin D can

Table 4 Foods High In Calcium		
Food	Weight or Measure	Calcium (Milligrams)
Plain nonfat and low-fat yogurts	8 oz./225g	350–450
Dry nonfat milk	1 oz./25g	350–450
Nonfat and low-fat milks	8 fl.oz	250–350
Swiss cheese	1 oz./25g	250–350
Hard cheeses such as Cheddar and Edam	1 oz./25g	150–250
Salmon, with bones	3 oz./80g	150–250
Collard greens	3 oz./80g	150–250
Soft cheeses such as mozzarella, blue and feta	1 oz./25g	50–150
Cooked dried beans such as navy, pea, and lima	3 oz./80g	50–150
Turnip greens, kale	4 oz./110g	50–150
Cottage cheeses	4 oz./110g	50–150
Broccoli	3 oz./80g	50–150
Orange	1 fresh	50–150
Dates, raisins	1 oz./25g	20–50
Bread, whole-wheat	1 slice	20–50
Cabbage	3 oz./80g	20–50

place an older person at risk for a vitamin D deficiency unless dietary sources are adequate. The only reliable source of this vitamin is vitamin D-fortified milk; other dairy products are not fortified with the vitamin. Sufficient amounts of vitamin D can be obtained each day from one quart of milk, by frequent exposure to sunlight, or through supplements. Vitamin D can be toxic and no more than 50 μg should be consumed on a regular basis.

Regular exercise is important to the maintenance of healthy bones. Exercise such as walking, jogging, or rope skipping puts pressure on the bones and increases the deposition of calcium into bones, which thickens and strengthens the bone tissues.

Cancer And Nutrition

Many forms of cancer are affected by diet. Between 35% and 60% of cancers are thought to be related to diet. Cancer of the breast, colon, uterus, ovaries, and prostate are linked to low-fibre and high-fat consumption. Besides fat and fibre, other dietary components are related to cancer.

Vitamin C, vitamin E, and selenium are nutrients that protect cells from damage and possible cancer. These nutrients either protect cell membranes from damage from highly reactive compounds called free radicals that might initiate cancer or they inhibit the formation of cancer-causing substances.

Consumption of vitamin C-rich foods is associated with a lower incidence of stomach and oesophageal cancer. In addition to protecting cell membranes, vitamin C neutralises some substances in food that might promote cancer. Vitamin C is also essential to a healthy immune system, which might defend the body against cancer-causing agents.

Vitamin E protects tissues from cancer-causing free radicals in polluted air and cigarette smoke. Vitamin E also might inhibit the growth of certain tumours.

Selenium works with vitamin E to protect cell membranes. Selenium also might strengthen the immune system. Patients with cervical and endometrial cancers are found to have low blood levels of selenium. The amount of selenium in the diet depends on the selenium content of the soil in which the food is grown. Seafood, meat, poultry, eggs, and whole grains are the most reliable sources of selenium.

Another nutrient that might protect a

person from developing cancer is vitamin A. Two forms of vitamin A exist. Retinol is the active form of vitamin A found in foods from animal sources such as offal, eggs, and milk products. Foods from plant sources contain beta-carotene, which is converted into vitamin A in the body. A diet high in beta-carotene-rich fruits and vegetables appears to decrease the risk of lung cancer. Several studies show a relationship between vitamin A intake and a reduced incidence or growth of cancers.

The form of vitamin A found in foods from animal sources and from some supplements is toxic in high doses. Liver damage, skin and bone problems, head-aches, and even death can occur if very large doses are taken over long periods of time. Beta-carotene, the source of vitamin A found in plants, is not toxic, although large doses will temporarily turn the skin yellow. Consume two or more servings of foods rich in beta-carotene each day. Dark green leafy vegetables and deep yellow and orange fruits and vegetables are high in beta-carotene.

Vegetables in the cabbage family might protect an individual from developing cancer. Leading experts in nutrition recommend frequent consumption of cabbage, broccoli, cauliflower, and Brussels sprouts.

Consumption of smoked and cured meats, salt-cured foods, pickled foods and alcohol, all of which contribute to cancer risk, should be limited.

Cardiovascular Disease

Cardiovascular disease (CVD) is a major cause of death and it is linked to diet and lifestyle. Several factors are involved in the development of CVD including a family history of heart disease, male gender, smoking, diabetes, overweight, stress, lack of exercise, high blood pressure, and a diet high in saturated fat and cholesterol.

Blood flow is reduced and the oxygen and nutrient supply to the tissues declines when fatty deposits of cholesterol build up in blood vessels. This process is called atherosclerosis. High amounts of cholesterol in the blood are associated with a greater risk for developing atherosclerosis. The clogged blood vessels in this disease increase the likelihood of a heart attack or stroke.

A diet high in fibre and complex carbohydrates and low in fat and sugar lowers blood levels of cholesterol and might slow or prevent the atherosclerotic process.

It is never too late to make changes in diet and exercise habits that can reduce the likelihood of developing CVD. It is recommended that people consume no more than 30% of their calories as fat and no more than 300 mg of cholesterol a day. Sugar should account for only 10% of the total calories and starchy foods should make the major contribution to the diet.

One dietary fat might protect a person from developing CVD. Eicosapentaenoic acid (or EPA) is a polyunsaturated fat found in fish. EPA might lower blood cholesterol and reduce the risk of developing CVD. Several servings a week of EPA-rich foods such as salmon, mackerel and sardines would provide a good supply of EPA.

Some types of fibre lower cholesterol and reduce the risk for developing CVD. Oatmeal, fruits, vegetables, and dried beans and peas contain the type of fibre that can lower cholesterol. A diet composed of whole, unprocessed foods such as fresh fruits and vegetables, dried beans and peas, whole grain breads and cereals, and low-fat milk products provides the best dietary health protection from CVD.

High Blood Pressure: One in every five people develops hypertension (high blood pressure) and one in every two people age 65 to 75 years old suffer from it. Hypertension increases the risk of developing CVD and kidney disease.

The best prevention against hypertension is to reduce the amount of salt and fat in the diet, maintain normal body weight, and consume an adequate amount of calcium. Often a reduction in weight alone lowers blood pressure. Calcium supplements can lower blood pressure in some individuals. Adequate intake of potassium and a reduction in salt also might reduce blood pressure. A diet low in total fat with a greater amount of fat from vegetable oils than from foods from animal sources might lower blood pressure. (*Figure 6, Page 56*)

Colds And Infections

Infections and colds can increase in the elderly, especially if disease is present. The immune system responds less efficiently

Figure 6. Sodium Content Of Selected Food (in mg)

 Apple
2

 Apple sauce
8 oz/225g
6

 Apple Pie
1/8, frozen
208

 Chicken
1/2 breast
69

 Chicken Pie
Frozen
907

 Chicken Dinner
Fast food
2,243

 Corn
1

 Corn Flakes
256

 Canned Corn
6 oz./170g
384

 Pork
3 oz./80g
59

 Bacon
4 slices
548

 Ham
3 oz./80g
1,114

 Potato
5

 Potato Chips
10
200

 Instant Mashed
6 oz./170g
485

 Tomato
14

 Tomato Soup
8 fl.oz
932

 Tomato Sauce
8 fl.oz.
1,498

 Tuna
3 oz./80g
50

 Canned Tuna
3 oz./80g
384

 Tuna Pot Pie
Frozen
715

 Water
8 fl.oz.,
tap
12

 Club Soda
8 fl.oz.
39

 Antacid*
In water
*Sodium bicarbonate
564

with age. Nutrition is important in strengthening the immune system. Nutrients of particular importance are protein, the vitamin B complex, vitamin C, vitamin A, vitamin E, iron, copper, selenium, and zinc. A nutritious diet of unprocessed foods from all the food groups is essential to protect against colds and infections. Equally important is consuming enough calories, since one of the most common forms of malnutrition in older adults is inadequate calorie intake.

Diabetes

Incidence of diabetes is high among the elderly, with 15% to 20% affected. In diabetes, glucose levels in the blood are high because glucose cannot enter the tissues. In addition to depriving the tissues of energy, high blood glucose causes severe health complications, which include kidney disease, impaired vision, cataracts, and heart disease.

Controlling blood sugar levels is important in older adults to prevent the serious problems of diabetes. Most adult diabetics can control their blood glucose levels with oral medications and diet. For many elderly people, however, dietary control is difficult. Arthritis, tremors, and physical weakness make it hard to shop for and prepare food. Eating is difficult with dental problems and diminished senses of taste, smell, and sight make eating less pleasurable. All these factors contribute to poor eating habits. Poor kidney function, infections, cancer, medications, and physical inactivity all upset the blood sugar balance.

Most people who develop diabetes later in life are overweight. Weight reduction is the first and most important step in controlling adult-onset diabetes. A healthy body weight often returns the glucose metabolism to normal and no other steps are needed. In other cases a nutritious diet high in fibre and complex carbohydrates (starch) is needed. Both fibre and complex carbohydrates help stabilise blood glucose. Since concentrated sweets do the opposite they need to be limited.

Adequate dietary chromium (50 μg to 200 μg/day) helps regulate blood sugar and might be an effective aid in the treatment for adult-onset diabetes. Good sources of chromium include whole wheat bread and whole grain cereals, brown rice, vegetables, and nutritional yeast. High chromium yeast supplements are also available.

Digestive Disturbances

The digestive processes can slow as a person ages. Adjustments in nutritional habits are important to reduce discomfort and avoid health problems. Serious health conditions can mimic common digestive disorders; gall-bladder disease, hiatal hernias, spastic colon, colitis (inflammation of the colon), and ulcers can produce feelings and symptoms similar to simple digestive disturbances. If digestive upsets persist, a physician should be consulted.

Constipation: Many people suffer from constipation at one time or another. Frequent occurrence is uncomfortable and also leads to more serious problems, such as haemorrhoids and diverticular disease. A diet that consists of processed and refined foods, such as white breads and cereals, white rice, and sugary foods, and is low in fresh fruits, vegetables, and dried beans and peas can contribute to chronic constipation in older adults.

A high-fibre and low-fat diet is essential to avoid constipation. The type of fibre found in whole wheat bread and whole grain cereals is most effective. Bran or oat bran sprinkled on cereal, or added to soups, stews, and casseroles can help relieve symptoms of constipation. Fibre from vegetables such as carrots, celery, and potatoes is also useful. Fluid consumption should be increased. Fresh fruits and vegetables add both fibre and fluid to the diet. A glass of prune juice, lemon juice in warm water, or other warm drink in the morning might be helpful.

In addition to diet, exercise improves muscle tone and the muscular activity of the digestive tract. Moderate physical activity such as daily walks helps digestive problems.

Overuse of laxatives is common among older adults and can be harmful. The laxative mineral oil binds to the fat-soluble vitamins A, D, E, and K in the intestine and increases their excretion. Mineral oil can cause deficiency of vitamin D, which contributes to the brittle bones of osteoporosis. Vitamin A deficiency adds to risk of cancer, poor eyesight, and also skin problems. Lack of vitamin K leads to easy bruising and bleeding problems.

Because of the potential for dependency on laxatives, treatment for constipation should combine a high-fibre diet, plenty of fluids, and regular exercise. Individuals should avoid chronic use of laxatives. If constipation persists, a physician should be consulted.

Heartburn: Heartburn is a burning, uncomfortable sensation in the middle chest that occurs after meals. The heart itself is not involved, but rather the oesophagus, which is the passageway between the throat and stomach. A small muscle at the bottom of the oesophagus, called the sphincter, weakens and acidic stomach juices backflow into the oesophagus. Some foods cause the sphincter muscle to open. These include spearmint and peppermint, coffee (regular and decaffeinated), fatty and fried foods, spicy foods, peppers, tomatoes, salad dressings, tomato and orange juices, radishes and alcohol. Overeating and smoking a cigarette after meals also lead to heartburn.

Heartburn can be controlled by eating small meals low in fat and high in both protein and carbohydrate. Maintenance of ideal weight can reduce the pressure placed on the muscle that leads to the oesophagus and might improve symptoms of heartburn.

Flatulence: The formation of excessive gas is caused by the following:

1. swallowing air while eating,
2. increased rate of movement of food in the intestine, or
3. excessive bacterial digestion of foods in the intestine.

Eating while relaxed and taking time to thoroughly chew food can reduce the amount of air swallowed.

A sudden increase in fibrous foods in the diet can speed the transport of undigested products through the intestine. The normal production of gases during the digestion of foods is usually absorbed through the walls of the intestine and dispersed in the blood. But when foods move too quickly through the intestinal tract these gases do not have time to disperse. A gradual increase in fibre intake over a few weeks allows the intestines time to adapt and might reduce the formation of intestinal gases.

Adults with intolerance to the milk sugar

lactose experience gas if they drink milk. This is a result of undigested milk sugar being broken down by bacteria in the intestine and the production of gases. Small amounts of milk often can be tolerated without discomfort.

Several foods tend to increase the production of intestinal gas including all carbonated drinks, whipped cream, dried beans and peas, cabbage, onions, and wheat. The gas-producing potential of beans is reduced by soaking them before cooking, discarding the water, and consuming these foods in small amounts.

Diverticulosis: A diet adequate in fibre also appears to prevent diverticulosis, a condition in which small pockets protrude from the colon wall and become infected and inflamed. Diverticulosis is most common in affluent, industrialised countries where the diet is high in meat, fat, and sugar and low in fibre.

Diverticulosis seldom develops before the age of 40, which suggests that the results of a low-fibre diet take years to develop. Excessive pressure from constipation causes pouches in the intestinal wall to develop. In contrast, fibre increases the stool size. This expands the diameter of the colon, reduces pressure in the colon wall, and prevents diverticulosis from developing.

Colon Cancer: A low-fibre, high-fat diet might contribute to the risk of developing colon cancer. People who consume low-fat diets have low rates of colon cancer. In response to a high-fat meal, bile is released into the intestine. Though useful for digestion, this bile also might generate cancer-causing substances in the intestine. Excessive dietary fat stimulates increased secretion of bile after a meal and might increase the risk of cancer. Fat also might encourage the growth of cancer-causing bacteria in the intestine.

Fibre is also useful in the prevention of cancer. Some bacteria in the intenstine produce cancer-causing substances. Fibre dilutes the contents of the intestine and reduces the effects of cancer-causing substances. Fibre also binds bile lessening its cancerous effects. Like fat, fibre also influences bacteria in the colon, but while fat promotes the harmful populations of bacteria, fibre promotes beneficial ones.

Oral Health

Several factors related to oral health can interfere with proper nutrition. For example, osteoarthritis in the jaw and gum inflammation from poorly fitting dentures can make chewing difficult. Osteoporosis and smoking both contribute to loss of teeth and by the age of 65, half of Americans have lost their teeth. To retard loss of calcium from the jaw bone and reduce the risk for loss of teeth, the diet should contain ample amounts of calcium, vitamin D, magnesium, and protein.

For people with poor-fitting dentures or lost teeth, vegetables, fruits, nuts, and lean meats can be difficult to chew. These foods are excellent sources of fibre, protein, vitamins, and minerals and their inclusion in the diet is important to health and the prevention of disease. These foods can be cooked, chopped, puréed, included in soups and stews, or cut into small bite-sized pieces for easy chewing.

Taste and smell diminish over the years and food might taste bland, bitter, or sour. A zinc deficiency also can cause changes in taste and inclusion of more zinc-rich foods in the diet, such as seafood, whole grain products, and milk, might improve the taste and appeal of foods. In addition, a small amount of a strongly flavoured food at the beginning of a meal can stimulate tastebuds, saliva flow, and interest in eating. The addition of more spices during cooking and at the table can improve the flavour of foods. An attractive table-setting and appetising appearance and texture of food can also improve a person's appetite.

Weight Control

Maintenance of a normal body weight helps prevent high blood pressure, diabetes, cancer, gall-bladder disease, arthritis, and cardiovascular disease. Over one-half of elderly women and nearly two-fifths of elderly men are obese. Overweight people are less active and show reduced physical fitness, stamina, energy, and mental health. Underweight, on the other hand, also shortens life and is associated with malnutrition.

Moderate exercise and a nutritious diet are the healthiest ways to lose weight. Activity increases metabolism and burns calories. Modest reduction in calories can help an individual lose fat weight, especially when combined with exercise.

Diets below 1,000 calories are ineffective for permanent weight loss. They slow metabolism, reduce burning of calories, and the weight lost is muscle rather than fat. A safe rate of weight loss is two to three pounds a week. More than this means muscle and fluid rather than fat is lost and the weight will be hard to keep

Table 5	Simple Menu For Weight Reduction (1,200 Calories)	
Breakfast Prune juice, 2 fl.oz. Cereal, fortified 2 oz./50g Nonfat milk, 8 fl.oz. Whole wheat toast, 1 slice Tea	**Lunch** Lean roast beef, 3 oz./80g Carrots, 3 oz./80g Rice, 3 oz./80g Fruit (fresh orange), 1 small Margarine, 1 tsp Coffee
Dinner Baked chicken, 3 oz./80g Cottage cheese, 4 oz./110g Tomato Lettuce Whole wheat bread, 1 slice Margarine, 1 tsp Fruit salad, 4 oz./110g	**Snack** Cantaloupe (melon), ¼ medium Nonfat milk, 8 fl.oz.

off. Losing and regaining the same 10 or 15 pounds is less healthy than maintenance of the extra weight. *(Table 5, Page 67)*

4

Medications And Nutrition

The elderly tend to use more medicines than other groups in the population, with a very large percentage of them regularly taking more than two medicines every day. Older adults are at high risk for nutritional problems. Frequent use of medications for chronic disease and minor complaints adds to the potential for nutrient deficiencies. As a person ages, medications are not metabolised as well and vulnerability to side effects increases. The use of several medications at once compounds the risk for nutritional deficiencies. Errors in dose can more easily occur in elderly people medicating themselves with several drugs.

Drugs interact with nutrition in the ways listed below:

1. Food can increase or decrease absorption of drugs,

2. Components of the diet change the rate of drug use in the body,
3. Drugs interfere with nutrient pathways, increase excretion, and change nutrient needs, and
4. Drugs affect appetite, taste, and food intake.

Antihistamines, steroids, tranquillisers, and anti-depressants can increase appetite and lead to weight gain. Several drugs, including alcohol and amphetamines, lower appetite and might lead to malnutrition. Digitalis and cancer drugs cause nausea and vomiting. D-penicillamine used to treat rheumatoid arthritis can lead to loss of taste, as can diuretics, antibiotics, anticancer drugs, and drugs used to treat Parkinson's disease and hypertension. Unpleasant taste changes might result in too little food intake and malnutrition.

Drugs that interfere with absorption of vitamins, such as colchicine, can impair vitamin B_{12} absorption and might lead to anaemia. Alcohol interferes with thiamin and folic acid absorption, which increases nerve problems and anaemia. Laxatives can produce deficiencies of the fat-soluble vitamins. The antibiotic neomycin has the same effect.

Other drugs lead to mineral depletion. Alcohol and some diuretics cause excretion of potassium, zinc, and magnesium. Regular use of aspirin causes the stomach to bleed, leading to iron deficiency and anaemia. Antacids can produce phosphate deficiency, leading to severe muscle weakness and convulsions.

These are just a few of the hundreds of drug-nutrient interactions. It is thus advised that anyone taking any drug on a regular basis should consult their doctor about the diet they should follow.

5

Nutrition And Ageing

Studies on centenarians show that a long life is associated with physical activity, close family ties, and sensible diets of fresh fruits and vegetables, whole grains, and little meat.

The consumption of a low-calorie diet also might improve chances for longevity. The earlier in life this type of diet is started, the longer the life. A diet low, but adequate, in protein and high in complex carbohydrates such as fruits, vegetables, and whole grain breads and cereals also might extend life.

Nutrition, health, and ageing are all closely connected. Chronic illness is now the cause of 80% of deaths. Dietary habits and weight control are an effective and essential means to prevent cancer, heart disease, osteoporosis, diabetes, and high blood pressure. A diet low in total fat, saturated fat, sugar, alcohol, and sodium and high in fibre and all nutrients is needed, with particular emphasis on adequate intake of vitamins A, E, C and D and the minerals calcium, chromium, and selenium.

The B vitamins are crucial to a healthy nervous system and alert mind. Protein, calories, and a wide range of vitamins and minerals keep the immune system strong. Chronic diseases also create new nutrient demands that can accelerate aging. Colds, infections, acute illnesses, and accidents require optimal nutrition in order to minimise sickness.

Exercise is essential to a healthy, long life. The advice to "use it or lose it" applies to the health of the heart, lungs, and circulatory system. Rather than wearing out the body, regular physical activity prevents it from deteriorating. Exercise also helps control chronic stress, which takes its toll on physical and mental health and increases risk of heart disease, cancer, high blood pressure, and diabetes.

Ageing is not a disease; it is a lifelong process and a natural part of the beauty and joy of life.

Appendix

The Nutrition Marketplace

Shopping And Cooking Tips

The following are some ideas to help over-
come common problems in shopping and
preparing food. Shopping for one or two:

- Buy small packages of items. Though
  sometimes more expensive, it is better
  than buying larger packages that spoil.
- Buy small amounts of fresh produce.
  Buy some that are ripe and some that
  will ripen in a day or two. Buy produce
  in season to avoid higher cost.
- Large bags of frozen vegetables are
  more economical than smaller packages. Remove what you need, seal, and
  return the bag to the freezer.
- When selecting whole grain breads,
  read the label; only those varieties that
  state "100% whole wheat" are certain

to contain whole wheat flour as their primary ingredient.

- Use dried skim milk powder in cooking. It is cheaper than fresh milk, stores longer, and works well for many uses. Sprinkle it into soups, sauces, and other dishes to boost calcium intake.
- Read ingredients labels on packaged foods. Avoid any foods that show fat or sugar as the first or second ingredient or that list different types of fat or sweeteners more than once.
- Ask for individual servings of lean meat to be wrapped rather than purchasing large packages of meat. If large packages of lean meat are purchased divide them into smaller portions, rewrap with foil or plastic, and store in the freezer. Loaves of bread also can be frozen.
- Keep staples on hand, such as tinned tuna, frozen vegetables, fruit juices, and cereal to avoid frequent shopping trips. *(Table 6, Page 77)*

How To Simplify Cooking:

- When cooking casseroles, soups, and stews, double the recipe and store one batch in the freezer or divide the dish into individual portions for reheating at a later time.

- Use leftover vegetables and meat in soup or stew.
- Sit down while preparing foods. Have a chair or stool of suitable height for the counters and stove.
- Keep pots and utensils within easy reach. If the cupboards are too low or too high for easy reaching, hang things on hooks or nails on the walls.
- Heat leftovers in one pan for easier cleaning.

When Choosing A Vitamin-Mineral Supplement Programme:

- Choose a supplement programme that provides the vitamins and minerals in amounts close to the RDA. The amount of a nutrient is expressed as a percent on the label. If the nutrient is at the level of the RDA it will say "100%."

Table 6 Shopping Wisely

Unwise Choice	Better Choice
Whole milk, sour cream, cream, nondairy creamers made with coconut or palm oil.	Low-fat or nonfat milk, evaporated nonfat milk.
Cream cheese, cheddar, and other whole milk cheeses.	Neufchatel cheese, low-fat cottage cheese, ricotta cheese.
Whole milk, fruited yogurt.	Plain, low-fat yogurt (add your own fruit).
Vegetables in sauces, vegetables, fruits in syrup, sweetened fruit juices.	Plain, fresh, or frozen vegetables, fresh or unsweetened fruits and juices, dried fruits.
Cakes, buns, doughnuts, sugar-coated or high sugar cereals, baking mixes, white rice.	Whole grain breads, rolls, crackers, flours and pastas, unsweetened whole grain cereals (oatmeal, shredded wheat, all bran etc), brown rice.
Beef with visible fat marbling, corned beef, bacon, sausage, breaded frozen seafood, tuna packed in oil, hot dogs, luncheon meats.	Chicken, turkey, plain fish, tuna packed in water, dry beans and peas, lean meat cuts (topside, sirloin steak, lean hamburger).
Peanut butter with hydrogenated oil added, salted nuts.	Unsalted "old-fashioned" peanut butter, unsalted raw nuts.
Ice cream, pastries, cakes, biscuits.	Sorbet, fruit.
Lard, coconut oil, palm, oil, hydrogenated or partially hydrogenated shortening, hard margarines.	Butter, safflower oil, corn oil, cornflower seed oil, soy oil, soft margarines, (USE ALL FATS & OILS SPARINGLY).

Glossary

Achlorhydria: The lack of sufficient stomach acid to digest foods.

Anaemia: A reduction in the number, size, or colour of red blood cells; results in reduced oxygen carrying capacity of the blood.

Antioxidant: A compound that protects other compounds or tissues from oxygen by reacting with oxygen.

Autoimmunity: A condition where the immune system attacks organs or tissues of the body as though they were foreign bacteria or substances.

Beta Carotene: The form of vitamin A found in plant foods such as carrots and dark green leafy vegetables.

Bile: A fluid secreted by the liver into the intestines that mixes with other secretions to digest fats.

Calorie: A measurement of heat. In nutrition, calorie refers to the quantity of energy contained in foods.

Cancer: The uncontrolled growth of abnormal cells.

Carbohydrate: The starches and sugars in the diet.

Cardiovascular Disease: A disease of the heart and blood vessels often caused by an accumulation of cholesterol in the lining of the blood vessels.

Cholesterol: A type of fat found in foods from animal sources and produced in the liver. High levels of cholesterol in the blood are associated with the development of cardiovascular disease.

Colitis: Inflammation of the colon, which is the lower portion of the intestine.

CVD: See Cardiovascular Disease.

Diabetes: A disorder in which the body's ability to use sugar is impaired because of inadequate production or utilisation of the hormone insulin.

Diuretic: An agent that increases the flow of urine.

Diverticulosis: Disorder of the colon associated with inflammation and the development of pouches.

Eicosapentaenoic Acid (EPA): A type of unsaturated fat found in fish that might lower blood levels of cholesterol and the risk for developing cardiovascular disease.

Endometrial: The lining of the uterus.

Enzyme: Protein-like substances in the body that initiate and accelerate certain chemical reactions.

Free Radical: A highly reactive compound derived from air pollution, radiation, cigarette smoke, or the incomplete breakdown of proteins and fats; reacts with fats in cell membranes and changes their shape or function.

Genetics: A branch of biology concerning heredity and biological variation.

Haemoglobin: The oxygen-carrying protein in red blood cells.

Hormone: A chemical substance produced by an organ called an endocrine gland, that is released into the blood and transported to another organ or tissue, where it performs a specific action. Examples of hormones are oestrogen, adrenalin, and insulin.

Hypertension: High blood pressure.

Immune System: A complex system of substances and tissues that protects the body from disease.

Lignin: A type of fibre found in some plant foods.

Metabolism: The sum total of all body processes, whereby the body converts foods into tissues and breaks down and repairs tissues and converts complex substances into simple ones for energy.

Obesity: Body weight more than 20% above desirable weight; excessive body fat.

Oesophagus: The passageway from the throat to the stomach.

Osteoporosis: Loss of calcium from the bones that results in porous, weak bones that are prone to fractures.

Prostaglandin: A group of hormone-like substances formed from fatty acids that have profound effects on the body, including contraction of smooth muscle and the dilation or contraction of blood vessels.

Prostate: An organ surrounding the neck of the bladder and the beginning of the urethra in males. This gland secretes a fluid that nourishes and hastens the movement of semen through the ure-thra.

Purine: Compounds in foods that might

aggravate the condition of gout. An example of a purine is uric acid.

Saturated Fat: A type of fat that is solid at room temperature and is found in foods from animal sources, hydrogenated vegetable oils, and coconut or palm oil. A diet high in saturated fats is linked to the development of cardiovascular disease and cancer.

Serotonin: A hormone-like substance produced in the brain that regulates mood, sleep, and numerous other body processes.

Stroke: Cerebrovascular accident caused by haemorrhage or a blood clot that blocks blood flow to a portion of the brain.

Tryptophan: An amino acid in the diet that the body uses to produce serotonin and the B vitamin niacin.

Unsaturated Fat: A type of fat that is liquid at room temperature and that is mainly found in foods of plant sources such as vegetable oils, nuts, and seeds.

Vitamins Checklist –
Needs and Sources

Vitamin A
Daily requirement
    adults   up to 1mg
    children   0.4mg rising to 1mg
Sources
    4oz./110g ox liver   6.8mg
    4oz./110g cooked
      carrots   2.25mg
    1 halibut liver oil capsule 1.2mg
    4oz./110g cooked
      spinach   1.15mg

Vitamin B1 (thiamin)
Daily requirement
    adults   1.25mg
    children   0.5mg rising to 1mg
Sources
    1oz./25g cereal +
      4fl.oz./½ cup semi-
      skim milk   0.4mg
    1 large slice of bread   0.15mg
    4oz./110g potato   0.1mg

Vitamin B2 (riboflavin)

Daily requirement

adults	1.5mg
children	0.8mg rising to 1.5mg

Sources

4oz./110g liver	3.5mg
6oz./160g cabbage or Brussels sprouts	1.5mg
1oz./25g cereal + 4fl.oz./½ cup semi-skim milk	0.6mg
1 egg	0.25mg

Vitamin B6 (pyridoxine)

Daily requirement

adults	2mg
children	1.5mg rising to 2mg

Sources

1 banana	480mg
1 orange	90mg
1 egg	50mg

NB Remember that Vitamin B6 is destroyed by heat, light and air.

Vitamin B12

Daily requirement

adults and children	3 micrograms

Sources

6oz./160g meat	2 micrograms
1oz./25g cereal + 4fl.oz./½ cup semi-skim milk	1 microgram
8fl.oz./1 cup milk	1 microgram

Folic Acid
Daily requirement
adults and children   400 micrograms
Sources
1 tablespoon brewers
     yeast   313 micrograms
4oz./110g cooked
     spinach   165 micrograms
6fl.oz. orange juice   102 micrograms
1oz./25g cereal +
     4fl.oz./½ cup semi-
     skim milk   80 micrograms

NB Remember that pregnant women, nursing mothers and women taking an oral contraceptive need extra folic acid.

Niacin
Daily requirement
men   18mg
women   13mg
children   6mg rising to 18mg
Sources
6oz./160g beef   12mg
1oz./25g cereal +
     4fl.oz./½ cup semi-
     skim milk   4.6mg
1oz./25g cheese   1.75mg
1 egg   1.65mg

Vitamin C
Daily requirement
adults   30mg–60mg
children   15mg–30mg

Sources
    4oz./110g fresh
        blackcurrants   220mg
    1 orange   60mg
    4oz./110g Brussels
        sprouts   40mg

Vitamin D
Daily requirement
    adults   10 micrograms
    children   7.5 micrograms
Sources
    cod liver oil capsule
        (check dose)   up to 10 micrograms
    1oz./25g cereal +
    4fl.oz./½ cup semi-
        skim milk   0.6 micrograms
NB Remember that much of the vitamin D
requirement is satisfied by exposure to normal
amounts of sunlight.

Energy and Minerals Checklist – Needs and Sources

Protein
Daily requirement
men	56 grams
women	44 grams

Sources
6oz./160g turkey	55 grams
8fl.oz./1 cup low fat milk	8 grams
1oz./25g cereal + 4fl.oz./ ½ cup semi-skim milk	6 grams
1 slice wholewheat bread	2.5 grams

Calories
Daily requirement
men	2,000 kcal
women	1,500 kcal

NB People taking strenuous physical exercise add up to 1,000 kcal

Sources
6oz./160g grilled steak	350 kcal
6oz./160g roast chicken without skin	24 0kcal
6oz./160g cod or haddock	120 kcal
6oz./160g chips	420 kcal
medium baked potato	150 kcal
1oz./25g slice of bread	70 kcal

1oz./25g butter	225 kcal
1oz./25g cheddar cheese	115 kcal
½pt./10fl.oz. pint semi-skim milk	125 kcal
1 chocolate digestive biscuit	85 kcal
½pt./10fl.oz. pint beer (bitter)	100 kcal
5fl.oz. dry white wine	95 kcal

Fibre

Daily requirement
adults and children   30 grams

Sources

1 orange	5.4 grams
1 medium baked potato	5.2 grams
1 slice wholewheat bread	2.7 grams
2 slices wholewheat crispbread	2.6 grams
1oz./25g bran flakes + 4fl.oz./½ cup semi-skim milk	2.5 grams

Calcium

Daily requirement

adults	500mg
teenagers and pregnant women	1,200mg

Sources

3oz./80g boiled spinach	500mg
8fl.oz./1 cup milk	300mg
1oz./25g cheese	250mg
1oz./25g cereal + 4fl.oz./ ½ cup semi-skim milk	160mg
1 tablespoon non-fat dried milk	52mg

Copper

Daily requirement
adults and children   2mg

Sources

6oz./160g ox liver	4.75mg
8fl.oz./1 cup whole milk	0.09mg

Iron
Daily requirement
    adults and children   12mg
Sources
    1oz./25g cereal + 4fl.oz./
        ½ cup semi-skim milk   2.1mg

Potassium
Daily requirement
    adults and children   2–3 grams
Sources
    1oz./25g cornflakes + 4fl.oz./
        ½ cup semi-skim milk   200mg
    1oz./25g oatmeal   111mg
    8fl.oz./1 cup whole milk   340mg

Sodium
Daily requirement
    adults and children   1–3 grams
Sources
    1 teaspoon salt   2.3 grams
    1oz./25g cornflakes + 4fl.oz./
        ½ cup semi-skim milk   400mg
    1oz./25g oatmeal   10mg
    7oz./200g baked beans   1 gram

Zinc
Daily requirement
    adults and children   10mg
Sources
    6oz./160g ox liver   7.2mg
    1oz./25g cheese   1.1mg
    8fl.oz./1 cup milk   0.93mg

Personal Nutrition Notes

Use this space to note the nutritional values of your own favourite foods. Do they make a valuable contribution to your diet?

Index

Laxatives, 60–61, 70–71
Liver disease, 36

Magnesium, 18, 32, 34, 35, 48, 65, 71
Medications, 16, 28, 44, 58, 69–71
  and appetite, 70
  and caffeine, 35, 36
  and folic acid, 30
Memory, 15, 17
  and vitamin B_{12}, 47
Menopause, 48
Metabolism, 14, 66, 67

Nails, 17
Nervous system, 13, 14
  and caffeine, 34–5
  and eyesight, 14
  and hearing, 14
  and vitamin A, 29
  and vitamin B_6, 46
Niacin, 18, 29, 45

Obesity, 19, 23, 53, 58, 66
Oedema, 25
Osteoarthritis, 65
Osteomalacia, 48
Osteoporosis, 8, 65, 72
  and calcium, 19, 25, 47, 48
  and exercise, 30
  and vitamin D, 19, 42, 60

Parkinsons disease, 70
Phosphate, 71
Polyunsaturated fats, 54
Potassium, 19, 35, 55, 71
Processed foods, 19, 22–3, 27, 53, 56

Prostaglandins, 43
Protein, 18, 20, 24–5, 32, 39, 44–7, 57, 61, 65, 73
Purines, 44

Respiratory disorders, 29
Retinol, 52
Rheumatoid arthritis, 41–3, 70

Salt *see* Sodium
Saturated fat, 26–7, 53, 73
Selenium, 43, 50, 51, 57, 73
Serotonin, 45, 46
Shopping, 74–5, 77
Skin, 14, 17, 25, 60–61
  and water, 33
Sleep, 35, 45, 46–7
Smell, 14, 15, 17, 20, 22, 58, 65
Smoking *see* Cigarette smoking
Sodium, 19, 22, 23, 34, 55, 56, 73
Spastic colon, 59
Stress, 11–12, 73
  and cancer, 73
  and CVD, 53, 73
  and diabetes, 73
  and exercise, 73
  and hypertension, 73
  and protein, 24–5
Stroke, 8, 53
Sugar, 19, 22, 23, 34, 54, 73

Taste, 14, 15, 17, 20, 22, 58, 65, 66
Tea, 34, 35, 36, 40
Teeth, 15, 19, 65
  and vitamin D, 19, 65